Bible reflections
for older people

BRF

The Bible Reading Fellowship
15 The Chambers, Vineyard
Abingdon OX14 3FE
brf.org.uk

The Bible Reading Fellowship (BRF) is a Registered Charity (233280)

ISBN 978 0 85746 782 9
All rights reserved

This edition © The Bible Reading Fellowship 2019
Cover image © Thinkstock

Acknowledgements

Scripture quotations marked BCP are taken from The Book of Common Prayer of 1662, the rights of which are vested in the Crown in perpetuity within the United Kingdom, and are reproduced by permission of Cambridge University Press, Her Majesty's Printers.

Scripture quotations marked NIV are taken from The Holy Bible, New International Version (Anglicised edition) copyright © 1979, 1984, 2011 by Biblica. Used by permission of Hodder & Stoughton Publishers, a Hachette UK company. All rights reserved. 'NIV' is a registered trademark of Biblica. UK trademark number 1448790.

Scripture quotations marked NRSV are taken from The New Revised Standard Version of the Bible, Anglicised edition, copyright © 1989, 1995 by the Division of Christian Education of the National Council of the Churches of Christ in the United States of America. Used by permission. All rights reserved.

'It Is Not Over' on page 34 © Ann Weems, from her collection *Kneeling in Bethlehem: Poetry for Advent and Christmas* (Westminster John Knox Press, 1993). Used with kind permission.

Every effort has been made to trace and contact copyright owners for material used in this resource. We apologise for any inadvertent omissions or errors, and would ask those concerned to contact us so that full acknowledgement can be made in the future.

A catalogue record for this book is available from the British Library

Printed and bound in the UK by Zenith Media NP4 0DQ

Contents

About the writers

Ann Lewin was a teacher of RE and English for 27 years. Now retired, she writes, leads quiet days and retreats, and works with individuals and groups, helping people explore their spirituality. She has had experience of caring for people living with dementia, first her mother and then one of her brothers, over a period of about 35 years.

Emlyn Williams worked for many years for Scripture Union, latterly for SU International, and spent much of his time with Christians in eastern Europe. He is a writer of many individual and group Bible materials and is currently Discipleship Pastor at a large Anglican church.

Roger Combes was a vicar in Hastings for 17 years after serving parishes in London and Cambridge. Before retiring, he served as an archdeacon in West Sussex. He and his wife live in Crawley. He has been a supporter of Bournemouth Football Club for 60 years, and still finds it slightly unbelievable that they are now playing in the Premier League.

Angela Tilby worked for the BBC as a producer of religious programmes for 22 years. Ordained in 1997, she became a tutor at Westcott House in Cambridge. After some years as a parish priest, she moved to Oxford as Diocesan Canon of Christ Church Cathedral. She writes for the *Church Times* and broadcasts frequently on Radio 4's *Thought for the Day*.

From the Editor

Welcome to this new collection of Bible reflections.

One of my all-time favourite films is *Ordinary People*, the 1980 American drama directed by Robert Redford and starring Donald Sutherland and Mary Tyler Moore. 'Ordinary' is a bit of a stretch, given the grandeur of the family home in which the tragic tale plays out, but it is a compelling film with stellar performances and it has stayed in my mind ever since I first saw it.

Two of our writers have focused on 'ordinary' people in the Bible, some of them so ordinary that they're not even named, unlike the stars who fill our cinema screens.

Another of our writers, the priest and one-time television film-maker Angela Tilby, shows that complex, sometimes tragic family dynamics and the timeless themes of love, lust, jealousy and greed are as prominent in the Bible and in 'ordinary' life as they are in glossy Hollywood dramas.

A much older Donald Sutherland recently starred as the patriarch J. Paul Getty in the television series *Trust*, exposing the dark underbelly of one of America's wealthiest and most dysfunctional families. It's a story that would sit convincingly in the Old Testament, but then so too could a touching tale of late-blooming love, released at about the same time: *Our Souls at Night* starred two lined but still beautiful octogenarians, Robert Redford and Jane Fonda.

God bless you

Using these reflections

Perhaps you have always had a special daily time for reading the Bible and praying. But now, as you grow older, you are finding it more difficult to keep to a regular pattern or find it hard to concentrate. Or maybe you've never done this before. Whatever your situation, these Bible reflections aim to help you take a few moments to read God's word and pray, whenever you have time or feel that would be helpful.

When to read them

You may find it helpful to use these Bible reflections in the morning or last thing at night, or any time during the day. There are 40 daily reflections here, grouped around four themes. Each one includes some verses from the Bible, a reflection to help you in your own thinking about God and a prayer suggestion. The reflections aren't dated, so it doesn't matter if you don't want to read every day. The Bible verses are printed, but if you'd like to read from your own Bible that's fine too.

How to read them

- **Take time** to quieten yourself, becoming aware of God's presence, asking him to speak to you through the Bible and the reflection.

- **Read** the Bible verses and the reflection:
  - What do you especially like or find helpful in these verses?
  - What might God be saying to you through this reading?
  - Is there something to pray about or thank God for?

- **Pray**. Each reflection includes a prayer suggestion. You might like to pray for yourself or take the opportunity to think about and pray for others.

Sing a new song

Ann Lewin

O come, let us sing unto the Lord... and show ourselves glad in him with psalms.

PSALM 95:1–2 (BCP)

All human life is reflected in the Psalms: joys and sorrows, hopes, fears and confusion. The people who wrote the psalms were not afraid to tell God what they were feeling, and they encourage us to be honest with God too.

The Psalms are sometimes referred to as the Jewish hymn book, but they would not have been used as we use hymn books, for there were no books as we know them, and most people would not have been able to read. The psalms were composed for particular occasions at different stages in the story of the Jewish people, to respond to situations, to accompany rituals, to express personal emotion. They would have been sung, and remembered through repetition.

The psalms are poetry, opening us up to explore new ways of understanding God and experiencing God's grace. Many of us have come to know the psalms through their use in worship over long years. Let's explore them together.

(The Bible quotations used in these reflections are taken from the Book of Common Prayer, which will be familiar to many. Some verse references may be slightly different to those you will find in other common translations.)

Psalm 118:24 (BCP)

Thanks for today

This is the day which the Lord hath made, we will rejoice and be glad in it.

Sometimes, as we grow older and life becomes complicated by physical, mental or emotional difficulties, we find ourselves wishing that life could be as it used to be: life when we were full of energy, never forgot what we had gone upstairs for and felt ourselves valued by those around us.

The psalmist says that kind of nostalgia won't help us to live today, for today is the day we are given by God. Rather than wishing it was something different, he suggests that we need to rejoice and be glad.

So we need to redirect our thinking, see what there is in our life today that can lift our spirits. It may be a fresh awareness of the beauty of the natural world; it may be a smile from a stranger; it may be a realisation of the blessings we are given by those who care for us. There are many things, great and small, which can make us thankful, an attitude to work at every day. As George Herbert wrote:

> *Not grateful when it pleaseth me*
> *As though thy blessings had spare days,*
> *But such a heart whose pulse may be*
> *Thy praise.**

■ PRAYER

'Lord, thou hast given so much to me, give one thing more, a grateful heart.'* Amen

* George Herbert, 'Gratefulnesse' (1633)

Psalm 92:1 (BCP)

Thanks for God's love

It is a good thing to give thanks unto the Lord.

'Count your blessings, name them one by one, and it will surprise you what the Lord has done,' sang Johnson Oatman in 1897.

There are many expressions of thanksgiving in the Psalms, and much encouragement to be thankful, corporately and alone. The psalmists were grateful for a whole range of things: the created world; God's faithful care of his people; our bodies (each one of us 'fearfully and wonderfully made', Psalm 139:14); good coming out of unpromising situations. There will be parallels to all these in our own lives.

Thankfulness puts life back into perspective when we are feeling sorry for ourselves. It does not always express what we are feeling – sometimes it is an act of the will, which needs to become habitual so that we can challenge the voices around or inside us that pull us towards despair about the world or about our own situation. Thankfulness is rooted in a recognition of the many blessings God gives us. There is no escaping the realities of life: the challenges and difficulties may well remain. We are not asked to be thankful for them, but to be thankful that in everything God's faithful love sustains us.

■ **PRAYER**

Loving God, thank you for your goodness, shown to us in so many ways. When life is hard, help us to remember that you are still faithfully holding us in your love. Amen

Psalm 69:30 (BCP)

A song of lament

When I am poor and in heaviness, thy help O God shall lift me up.

When life falls apart and God seems a long way away, the psalmists encourage us to lament. Lament is not moaning about how awful life is; it is describing what we are experiencing. Then the psalmists encourage us to put alongside our lament a statement about God, who is ultimately in control. We have to go on living in the space between the two.

Our feelings can be very raw and disturbing. Take wanting to get revenge, for example. We may well have been brought up to believe that Christians should love their enemies and not try to get their own back by giving as bad as we get. But if that is what we feel we would like to do, the psalmist encourages us to be honest with God and say so.

In doing this, we won't be telling God anything he doesn't know about us already, and nothing will stop God loving us. When we admit to our feelings, God can begin to give us new insights and work in us for change – if not by changing the situation, at least by changing our attitude towards it and those involved. We don't have to beat ourselves up about the desire for revenge or about any other negative feelings we sometimes have. Christians are not perfect; we are works in progress.

■ PRAYER

Loving God, help us to own our feelings honestly and open ourselves up to your transforming love. Amen

Psalm 84:5–6 (BCP)

Drink from the well

Blessed is the man whose strength is in thee: in whose heart are thy ways. Who going through the vale of misery, use it for a well: and the pools are filled with water.

Anyone's life can go through a time of upheaval, when things can look very dark indeed. At times like these, the psalmist says, we need to use the experience positively.

'You must be joking,' might be our response. How can we make sense of this, whatever it is, and use it? At times like these, we need to cling on to God, trusting that God won't let go. There are no quick fixes, and the darkness and difficulty may go on for some time, but we may find mysterious refreshment as we discover pools of God's love and grace and drink deeply from them.

We are more likely to be able to do this if we have spent time when life is going well building up our relationship with God. Prayer, Bible study and joining in worship all contribute to the growth of that relationship, which is a gift from God to all who open themselves up to receive it. It's never too late to start or to re-establish habits that we have allowed to fall into disuse.

■ **PRAYER**

Life-giving God, when our existence seems hardly worth living and problems seem insurmountable, fill us with hope and refresh us with your Spirit. Amen

Psalm 46:1–2 (BCP)

Do not fear

God is our hope and strength, a very present help in trouble.
Therefore will we not fear though the earth be shaken and though the
hills be carried into the midst of the sea.

Truth be told, most of us are afraid at least some of the time: the world seems to have gone mad. We don't think so much in the psalmist's terms of hills being carried into the midst of the sea, though the warnings about global warming and rising sea levels, and our experience of extreme weather conditions with hurricanes, droughts, tsunamis and floods bringing destruction, come quite close to them.

Tensions between super- and not-so-superpowers, the existence of military hardware that could destroy much of our world and the brutality with which people treat their fellow humans, both on an international scale and on our streets, can all make us wonder what the world is coming to.

This psalm reminds us that because of God's faithfulness, we need never be afraid.

Our prayer for today takes the form of words we often use at the end of a psalm, reminding us of the unchanging faithfulness of God. Our calling is to trust and to give God glory and praise whatever is going on around or within us.

■ PRAYER

Glory be to the Father, and to the Son, and to the Holy Ghost. As it was in the beginning, is now and ever shall be, world without end. Amen

Psalm 27:16 (BCP)

Be still

O tarry thou the Lord's leisure: be strong and he shall comfort thine heart: and put thou thy trust in the Lord.

'Wait and see' was one of the most infuriating things my mother used to say to me when I was little – usually when I wanted to know what was for pudding before I'd finished my main course.

Learning to wait is a valuable lesson, because as life goes on there are many times when we have to do so. Waiting goes against the grain of our culture: we live in a world that expects instant responses, which can sometimes come disastrously quickly.

Life itself is the product of waiting: for humans, the nine months in the womb can't be hurried, and if for any reason they are interrupted, either life is lost or premature birth puts normal growth at risk.

Spiritually, too, we need time to grow and get in tune with God's timetable. Could we, when perhaps time hangs heavy as we wait for appointments, test results or the arrival of carers, get into the habit of being still with God? Time spent with God is never wasted and is much more worthwhile than getting agitated over things we can't do anything about.

■ PRAYER

'God, grant me the serenity to accept things I cannot change, the courage to change the things I can, and the wisdom to know the difference.'* Amen

*Reinhold Niebuhr (1892–1971)

Psalm 103:1–2 (BCP)

Freedom to grow

Praise the Lord, O my soul: and all that is within me, praise his holy name. Praise the Lord, O my soul: and forget not all his benefits.

One of the benefits God gives us is forgiveness of all our sins. There are times when all of us wish we hadn't said or done something, or have let something wrong go on without challenging it. It's never too late to try to put things right – except that sometimes the people concerned have died, and we can't do anything about it. Going on feeling guilty doesn't help – it won't change anything and will only reinforce our feelings of inadequacy.

Some feelings of guilt are inappropriate because they are nothing to do with offending against God's law of loving God and our neighbour; they are the result of what authority figures told us was not acceptable as we were growing up. But there are things for which we are responsible, about which we rightly feel guilt and need to seek forgiveness for.

God's forgiveness doesn't mean that sin doesn't matter; God's forgiveness means that nothing we do or say can stop God loving us. God sets us free to forgive ourselves and move on. It's never too late for that.

■ PRAYER

Merciful God, help us to take hold of your forgiveness and to live in the freedom you offer us to grow and become what you long for us to be. Amen

Psalm 103:3–4 (BCP)

The new normal

[The Lord] healeth all thine infirmities… saveth thy life from destruction and crowneth thee with mercy and loving kindness.

The psalmist reminds us of more of God's benefits – healing and the blessing of life. We sometimes feel let down when we or others we are praying for don't get better. That may be because we confuse 'healing' with 'cure': the two are quite different.

Some conditions can be treated: toothache will disappear when the offending tooth is filled or extracted. Other conditions are more complex; treatment may alleviate the immediate problem, but it may not eradicate the cause. Life may be saved, but pain does not always disappear; we may have to learn to live with it. Healing doesn't mean going back to what we were like before the problem attacked us; it means going on to a new stage of being. Healing often happens at a deeper level than the obvious physical or mental conditions we can see – it is more like the establishment of a sense of well-being, which holds us steady whatever life throws at us.

Learning what that new stage is going to be takes time, but the psalmist assures us that God's love is going to support us as we discover what our 'new normal' is going to be.

■ **PRAYER**

God of life, thank you for bringing new opportunities out of dark and difficult experiences. Help us to hold on to you when we can't see the way forward. Amen

Psalm 23:4 (BCP)

God with us in death

Yea, though I walk through the valley of the shadow of death, I will fear no evil: for thou art with me.

As we grow older, we become more aware of our own mortality, as perhaps we experience life-threatening illness and almost certainly experience bereavement as our contemporaries die.

The psalms say little that is positive about death, because of the prevailing belief that there was nothing beyond it. But this psalm has encouraged people throughout the centuries to face death secure in the belief that God will hold them and they need not be afraid. Death will come, and an important element in preparing for it is to strengthen our relationship with the God who is going to be with us through the experience. We can do this by spending time regularly getting used to being in God's presence and taking all the opportunities we are given to enjoy the life we have. There are practical things to attend to as well, such as making a will and telling people where to find important documents.

Christians don't have any clearer idea than the Old Testament Jews did about what lies beyond death. But Jesus assured us that he was going through death to prepare a place for us to be in God's presence for eternity. Death is the beginning of new life.

■ **PRAYER**

Living God, keep alive in us the hope that your gift of eternal life will carry us through death into the fullness of your presence. Amen

Psalm 4:9 (BCP)

A peaceful night

I will lay me down in peace and take my rest: for it is thou, Lord, only that makest me dwell in safety.

I used to look forward to Zebedee's appearance in *The Magic Round-about*, as he sprang into the story with his catchphrase, 'Time for bed.'

It may be true that we don't need as much sleep as we get older, because we don't use up so much energy during our waking hours – though sleep often overtakes us in the course of the day. But realising that doesn't help us much when we lie in bed for ages, unable to sleep. Sometimes there is a reason for this: we are worried about something, or we are in pain. At other times, for no apparent reason, however much we try, sleep eludes us. This mysterious slide into oblivion is something over which we have no control: it is God's gift.

Instead of tossing and turning, let's remind ourselves that God is holding us safe, perhaps by repeating some verses we have come to treasure which assure us that we are safe with God, like these from Bishop Ken's hymn.

■ PRAYER

O may my soul on thee repose
and may sweet sleep my eyelids close;
sleep that may me more vigorous make,
to serve my God when I awake.
When in the night I sleepless lie,
my soul with heavenly thoughts supply;
let no ill dreams disturb my rest,
no powers of darkness me molest.* Amen

*Bishop Thomas Ken, 'All Praise to Thee My God This Night' (1695)

Sixty per cent water

Emlyn Williams

The title of the TV show *Pointless Celebrities* (the celebrity version of *Pointless*) always amuses me. It's a bit unfair, I know, because the celebrities are certainly not pointless people. All too often, however, I recognise neither their names nor their faces. Perhaps I'm just out of touch...

Some say that we're in a celebrity-obsessed world. The media is full of gossip about celebrities, and we seem to lap it up. Perhaps it gives those of us with much more ordinary lives a glimpse of what we might like our lives to be. Nevertheless, in the end we're all made of the same stuff – we're 60% water.

I suppose there's a danger of looking at Bible characters in the same way. There are many well-known heroes in the Bible – you can read about some of them in Hebrews 11. Their example is powerful. But there are many ordinary people whose lives made a difference too. Thankfully, their stories are also included in the Bible, and in this series we're going to meet some of them. We don't even know some of their names, but their stories live on. Let's see how God might speak to us through some ordinary lives.

Luke 2:15-17 (NIV)

Ordinary people

The shepherds said to one another, 'Let's go to Bethlehem and see this thing that has happened, which the Lord has told us about.' So they hurried off and found Mary and Joseph, and the baby, who was lying in the manger. When they had seen him, they spread the word concerning what had been told them about this child.

What are 'ordinary people'? We sometimes talk about 'the man in the street'. Lawyers have referred to 'the man on the Clapham omnibus'. Americans speak of an 'average Joe'. But whatever term we prefer, the reality is that most of us are ordinary. It doesn't mean that we're not valuable, just that there are lots of other people like us around.

The shepherds here were pretty ordinary – we don't even know their names. But in another way, they were anything but ordinary. The angel could have told all sorts of important, educated, even holy people about Jesus' birth. Instead, it was to these shepherds that the birth of the Saviour, Christ the Lord, was announced.

I guess the shepherds knew that they were ordinary, but it didn't stop them from talking about what they had been told. The baby in the manger could have been any baby. But the shepherds knew who he really was and spread the word.

■ PRAYER

Thank you, Lord, that you can speak through anyone, even ordinary people like the shepherds and like me. Please help me to share what I know about you with people I meet today. Amen

Luke 2:36–38 (NIV, abridged)

Just the right place

[Anna] was very old; she… was a widow until she was eighty-four. She never left the temple but worshipped night and day, fasting and praying. Coming up to [Mary and Joseph] at that very moment, she gave thanks to God and spoke about the child to all who were looking forward to the redemption of Jerusalem.

I went to an air show recently. When I arrived, it was a challenge to find my son among the thousands of people there; we ended up phoning each other. Meeting someone in the massive temple in Jerusalem would have been a similar challenge, even if you knew they were there. But Anna didn't know Mary and Joseph had arrived. I suspect that God had a hand in ensuring that they all met.

At her age – possibly over 100, as the verse could mean that she was a widow for eighty-four years – Anna might have been excused for losing her hope that the Messiah would come. She didn't. Her faithful worship, fasting and prayer over long years were rewarded. When the child arrived in the temple, she was there.

Are there things you've been praying and working for over many years? Be encouraged by Anna and keep going. Trust God to guide you to be in the right place at the right time.

■ **PRAYER**

Lord, thank you that I can entrust my longings and fears to you. May I have the perseverance to wait for the right place and the right time. Amen

John 6:5, 8–9 (NIV)

Every little helps?

When Jesus looked up and saw a great crowd coming towards him, he said to Philip, 'Where shall we buy bread for these people to eat?'… Andrew, Simon Peter's brother, spoke up, 'Here is a boy with five small barley loaves and two small fish, but how far will they go among so many?'

Have you seen the TV adverts – often on during the daytime – asking you to give just £3 per month to a charity? It seems like such a small amount: what possible difference could it make? Well, clearly those gifts can make a real difference.

Here in these verses, we read of someone who is young, unnamed and with the tiniest amount of food. Did he offer the food himself or did Andrew notice it and suggest that he give it? We don't know, but what is clear is that Jesus took that small gift and made something very significant of it.

It's so easy to feel that in a big world with huge problems, we can't make a difference. But it's not true. Jesus took the boy's tiny gift and multiplied it again and again. And there was still food left over. What small gift can you offer to God?

■ **PRAYER**

Thank you, Lord, for the example of this boy. Please show me today what I can do for you that will make a real difference in this needy world. Amen

Matthew 4:18–22 (NIV, abridged)

Left behind

[Jesus] saw two brothers, Simon called Peter and his brother Andrew... 'Come, follow me,' Jesus said... At once they left their nets and followed him. Going on from there, he saw two other brothers, James son of Zebedee and his brother John. They were in a boat with their father Zebedee, preparing their nets. Jesus called them, and immediately they left the boat and their father and followed him.

You may know people who have chosen to obey God by responding to a challenge to do something new or different. They may be overseas working with churches or the poor. They may have gone to serve God elsewhere in this country. But you may know from personal experience that this often has implications for family and friends left at home. Commenting on early Baptist missions, someone said it was 'the committed-here supporting the committed-there'.

The story of Jesus choosing the disciples is familiar to many of us. But it's interesting that here, Zebedee, father of James and John, gets a mention as well as his sons. When the two brothers answered Jesus' call, they didn't just leave their nets, but they also left Zebedee. Their obedience was costly for him, too. When we think of and pray for people serving God in exciting and perhaps risky ways, we also need to remember those they have left behind.

■ **PRAYER**

Do you know anyone who is missing a family member or friend because they have gone to serve God in another place or even overseas? Pray now that God will comfort and strengthen them.

1 Samuel 1:10–11a (NIV)

Please, God

In her deep anguish Hannah prayed to the Lord, weeping bitterly. And she made a vow, saying, 'Lord Almighty, if you will only look on your servant's misery and remember me, and not forget your servant but give her a son, then I will give him to the Lord for all the days of his life.'

Bargaining with God is an understandable temptation when you're desperate. I think, perhaps, we've all done it. Hannah wanted a son so much that she said that if God answered her prayer, she would give the child back to God for the rest of his life. That's how fraught she was. And things were so much worse because her husband Elkanah had another wife. Penninah seemed to be able to have children incredibly easily and, to make it worse, she taunted Hannah about it.

What Hannah didn't realise was that God had a much bigger purpose for her than she could ever imagine. Yes, he answered her prayer and gave her a son. And yes, Hannah was faithful to her vow, dedicating Samuel to the Lord and leaving him to be brought up in the temple to serve God. But he went on to become a priest, prophet and judge – one of the greatest ever. Had Hannah not had her problems, that would not have happened.

■ PRAYER

Father God, help me to trust you when things in my life are difficult. May I be able to see that your purposes are much bigger than I can realise. Amen

Exodus 1:15–17 (NIV, abridged)

Who do you obey?

The king of Egypt said to the Hebrew midwives, whose names were Shiphrah and Puah, 'When you are helping the Hebrew women during childbirth… if you see that the baby is a boy, kill him; but if it is a girl, let her live.' The midwives, however, feared God and did not do what the king of Egypt had told them to do; they let the boys live.

Some issues never go away, and obedience to God is one of them. The Egyptians were afraid that the Israelites might take over. So Pharaoh ordered the Hebrew midwives to kill the Israelite boys at birth. That way, the birth rate would decrease and the Israelite boys would not become a rival army. The future of Israel was literally in the hands of these 'ordinary' women, Shiphrah and Puah.

The midwives faced a dilemma. Should they obey Pharaoh? Or should they do what God wanted? Although they were putting themselves in danger, they disobeyed Pharaoh and let the boys live.

Have you ever had to disobey someone in authority because you believed they were wrong? Perhaps that was very painful and you paid the price. In the case of these midwives, there was a happier ending. God honoured them and gave them families of their own.

■ PRAYER

Thank you for 'ordinary' people like Shiphrah and Puah, who were willing to do the right thing regardless of the cost. Please be with those who are facing the challenge of loyalty to you, even today. Amen

Luke 23:39–43 (NIV, abridged)

Never too late

*One of the criminals who hung there hurled insults at [Jesus]…
But the other criminal rebuked him. 'Don't you fear God?' he said…
'We are… getting what our deeds deserve. But this man has done
nothing wrong.' Then he said, 'Jesus, remember me when you come
into your kingdom.' Jesus answered him, 'Truly I tell you, today you
will be with me in paradise.'*

One of my relatives, after a lifetime of seeming to ignore God,
prayed for forgiveness. Soon afterwards, he died. Was he genuine?
Or was he hedging his bets 'just in case'? This story, one of the
most hopeful – and shortest – in the Bible, challenges that doubt.
An unnamed criminal, dying on a cross, is told by Jesus that he will
join him in paradise that same day. No ifs, no buts. And my relative's
prayer was just as valid and just as acceptable to God.

To many, this seems very unjust: why should God accept someone
who has ignored him all their life? But that misses the point. No one
is accepted by God because they have done the right things. God
accepts us because of what Jesus has done. That's why it is just.
'Everyone who calls on the name of the Lord will be saved' (Romans
10:13).

■ **PRAYER**

*Spend some moments thanking God that faith rests on what Jesus
has done and not on our goodness. Pray for people you know who
seem not to have understood that truth, that they will turn to him.*

2 Kings 5:1–3 (NIV, abridged)

I know a man who can

Naaman was commander of the army of the king of Aram… He was a valiant soldier, but he had leprosy. Now bands of raiders from Aram had gone out and had taken captive a young girl from Israel, and she served Naaman's wife. She said to her mistress, 'If only my master would see the prophet who is in Samaria! He would cure him of his leprosy.'

Do you remember the old TV commercial for the AA, where the children asked their dad if he could fix their broken-down car? 'No,' he replied, 'but I know a man who can!' Well, here the roles are reversed, and it's a child who knows a man who can. A senior military officer, Naaman, had a terrible skin disease. His wife's young Israelite servant – in effect a prisoner of war – heard about his leprosy. She said that she was sure that Elisha the prophet would be able to cure him.

To Naaman's credit – or perhaps out of desperation – he was humble enough to follow her advice and Elisha's instructions. Not only was he healed, but he also came to believe that 'there is no God in all the world except in Israel' (2 Kings 5:15). Often we want to fix problems but we can't – but if we point people to the one who can, the Lord, we have done our part.

■ PRAYER

Thank you, Lord, that when we can't, you can. Please help me today to have the courage to point people in need to you for help. Amen

1 Chronicles 4:9–10 (NIV)

The God who answers

Jabez was more honourable than his brothers. His mother had named him Jabez, saying, 'I gave birth to him in pain.' Jabez cried out to the God of Israel, 'Oh, that you would bless me and enlarge my territory! Let your hand be with me, and keep me from harm so that I will be free from pain.' And God granted his request.

Some names are descriptive even if they're not quite accurate. Will Mrs Cook win *Masterchef*? Is Mr Lamb always gentle? Jabez had a name with an apt meaning. In Hebrew it sounds like 'pain', which is what his mother said about his birth.

These verses tell us everything we know about Jabez. He had brothers but, alone among the many named in this chapter, he was fatherless, an outsider with no place in the land. In effect, he was a refugee – no wonder he asked God for land, to 'enlarge [his] territory'.

There is nothing special about his prayer, despite the suggestion made in a controversial bestseller some years ago. But it is a good prayer, reminding us that God hears our prayers and answers them.

As for his name, it was not the final word about Jabez. Pain may have surrounded the start of his life, but not the end. Through God there was a way out of his circumstances, and that's just as true for us.

■ **PRAYER**

Lord, give me the confidence to bring my needs to you and the faith to wait for your answer. Amen

John 4:46–50a (NIV, abridged)

Desperation

Once more he visited Cana in Galilee… A certain royal official whose son lay ill at Capernaum… went to [Jesus] and begged him to come and heal his son, who was close to death. 'Unless you people see signs and wonders,' Jesus told him, 'you will never believe.' The royal official said, 'Sir, come down before my child dies.' 'Go,' Jesus replied, 'your son will live.'

24 Hours in A&E is a gripping TV series. Over and over, we see desperate relatives rushing to be with their seriously ill family. The fear and dread brought by not being with them is palpable.

Twenty miles from Cana, a boy is dying, and his father has come to Jesus for help. Imagine his desperation. His status and wealth won't help. He asks Jesus to come with him before it's too late. So how do you think he felt when Jesus simply told him to go home because the boy would live?

But 20 miles away, at that very same moment, the boy got better. Jesus didn't have to rush there with a police escort. His power wasn't restricted by geography. Only after the overnight trip home did the father discover that his trust in Jesus had been well-placed.

■ **PRAYER**

Lord Jesus, we don't know the name of the father, but we remember his faith in you. Help us to follow his example of trust, whether or not we're in desperate straits at the moment. Amen

The Gift of Years

Debbie Thrower is the Pioneer of BRF's Anna Chaplaincy for Older People ministry, offering spiritual care to older people, and is widely involved in training and advocacy.

Visit **annachaplaincy.org.uk** to find out more.

Debbie writes…

Welcome! The older I get, the more I recognise a tendency to stoop; too much time spent in a sedentary role, I expect. A photo of my grandmother, though, on a stage accepting an award in her later years shows her with a marked bent back, so perhaps it runs in the family?

As we age, our bodies bear traces of our habits and life experiences, as well as our genetic inheritance. It's striking that Jesus bore the marks of being nailed to the cross in his risen body.

I hope you find these reflections inspiring, as I do, for the way they contrast the ordinariness of us all with the extraordinary story of humankind being continually sought out by God. The fact that, in the Christmas story particularly, God stooped down to become 'one of us' is truly humbling.

Blessed art thou
O Christmas Christ,
that thy cradle was so low
that shepherds
poorest and simplest of earthly folk
could yet kneel beside it,
and look level-eyed into the face of God.
Anonymous, from *The Christmas Stories* (SPCK, 2007)

Best wishes

Meet the writer: Ann Lewin

 **Ann Lewin** was a teacher of RE and English for 27 years and then welfare advisor for international students at the University of Southampton. In retirement she writes, occasionally leads quiet days and retreats, and works with individuals and groups, helping people explore their spirituality. She is best known for her poem about prayer, 'Watching for the Kingfisher', and the bestselling book named after it. Born in Southampton three years before the beginning of World War II, she remained in the city through her childhood and young adult years, only leaving after university when she moved to Exeter to complete her postgraduate teaching certificate. From her earliest days, church was a big part of her life. She says:

We were a very convinced churchgoing family. When the war began, churches had to be blacked out like every other building, but we couldn't black out our church, so the evening services moved to the afternoon. That meant that my parents could go to church together with me; my brothers were in the choir. So from the age of three, I've had Evensong wafting over me. I'm told I used to sing 'All Things Bright and Beautiful' whatever anyone else was singing. Belonging to a church has been part of me right from the start.

You taught English and RE?

Yes, it was RE to start with and then English was added, partly because as the RE teacher I was teaching everyone in the school for one lesson a week, which meant that I could never really build relationships with the students; a lot of them thought RE was a waste of time anyway. I wanted to be with young people in a different way, so I started teaching English as well. Teaching for me has always been about opening people's eyes and stretching their horizons: opening them up to new ways of looking at things.

What about your writing – have you always written?

Yes, I've always written. I've always enjoyed using words, but the kind of things that have been published emerged quite late on. I'd never thought of 'being a writer'. It was at one of the turning points in my life when I started exploring what I was feeling in words. Then shortly afterwards, I found myself being a carer for my mother with dementia and I started writing about that. I wrote a series of poems called 'Mother Care', which are reflections on the experience of looking after someone with dementia, and when I showed them to a few friends they said, 'You must share this with others.'

I produced a little pamphlet of poems, including the 'Mother Care' sequence and a few others as well, called 'Unfinished Sentences'. It came out just before Christmas in 1987. I sold it for a pound and the copies all went and people asked me for more. So I compiled two or three collections, taking pieces that had already been published and adding to them. No publisher wanted to publish what I had written, because they said there was no demand for it, so I went down the route of self-publishing.

Eventually Methodist Publishing got interested and began publishing my work to stop it going out of print, because I could no longer afford to self-publish, and then they too went out of business and Canterbury Press came to be my publisher. But that all happened without me once thinking, 'Oh, I'm going to be a writer.'

How do you feel about being known mainly for one exquisite poem?

I'm absolutely delighted because I think it says something about prayer that is important for people to know: prayer is a gift, like seeing a kingfisher. The important thing is to be there, to be ready, expectant, looking to meet God, to let God meet you. Just as you can't make a kingfisher come, you can't make God do anything either. So when prayer is hard, you just have to stay with it, like birdwatchers do, and see what happens.

There's a newspaper column called 'This I have learned', which invites people to share the wisdom they've gleaned over the years. What have you learned?

What I've learned over the years is that age is not all about loss and diminishment. Psalm 92 is one of my favourites because it ends up by saying that people can still bear fruit in their older years. I think that growing older is a time for that kind of fruitfulness: over the years, we have acquired some wisdom which is valuable and worth sharing. It's a gift we're given through the experiences we have, so I would say that growing older is a positive, though it also has some pretty challenging aspects to it: it's certainly not for wimps, as people say. Underlying all my experience is my conviction that God is faithful and will not let us go.

Sister Pia Buxton CJ

 Eley writes: Sister Pia Buxton CJ was a much-loved and highly respected spiritual director and retreat-giver, who has been sadly missed since her death in 2010. She loved poetry and literature and always at her feet, as she listened to directees, sitting tall in her armchair, concentrating intently, was a bulging concertina file of poems and quotations. Sister Pia knew every last treasure in that file and at exactly the right moment would bend to ruffle through myriad slips of photocopied paper – different shapes, colours and sizes – until she found the perfect words to give to the person she was accompanying.

Her favourite poets were Mary Oliver, Ann Lewin (who features in this issue of Bible reflections) and the Presbyterian elder and lecturer, Ann Weems.

She used to tape a copy of Mary Oliver's poem 'Why I Wake Early' to the front door of the retreat house in Whitby, where she spent a month every summer, and one Christmas she slipped a copy of Ann Weems' poem 'It Is Not Over' into her Christmas cards. I've loved this poem ever since, and I'm grateful to the publishers for allowing us to share it with you. And I love the fact that, unknowingly, Angela Tilby, in one of the last reflections for this year, almost quotes the poem when she writes, 'Christ has ever new ways of showing us we are saved from our sins.'

I hope you enjoy 'It Is Not Over' as much as I do.

It Is Not Over

It is not over,
*   this birthing.*
There are always newer skies
*   into which*
*   God can throw stars.*
When we begin to think
*   that we can predict the Advent of God,*
*   that we can box the Christ*
*   in a stable in Bethlehem,*
*   that's just the time*
*   that God will be born*
*   in a place we can't imagine and won't believe.*
Those who wait for God
*   watch with their hearts and not their eyes,*
*   listening*
*   always listening*
*   for angel words.*

Ann Weems, from her collection *Kneeling in Bethlehem: Poetry for Advent and Christmas* (Westminster John Knox Press, 1993). Used with kind permission.

It was an ordinary morning

Anne Townsend

 My mother, Dr Barbara Cawthorne, went to south India to marry a missionary. I was a honeymoon baby. Because this was before antibiotics and modern antimalarials were available, missionary babies were dying and, reluctantly, they came back to the UK, where they had three more children. Among her many claims to fame, Barbara was a member of the first Anglican General Synod in 1970 and she learned to scuba dive in her 60s before wetsuits were invented. When she died, aged 102, she was remembered on BBC Radio 4's *Last Word*. I also became a medical missionary, in Thailand, and went on to become a priest and psychotherapist, as well as a popular writer. Here, I remember an extraordinary encounter.

It was an ordinary morning. Ordinary things were happening all around us. Workers munched their way through their bacon butties. Buses and vans swerved round the pavement, heading for the congested A3 road. The sun shone its feeble best. Enthroned in her wheelchair on the pavement by Jake's Burger Bar, my 101-year-old mother was savouring her customary mug of strong builder's tea. No one realised that something totally extraordinary was about to happen.

Out of the corner of my eye, I noticed a man in his late 60s, moving slowly across the grass, his eyes glued to the ground, as if searching for hidden treasure. But no treasure was to be found. His task was to collect every scrap of litter scattered on the grass and pavements. He focused intensely, as if his life depended on this.

Our eyes met and we exchanged smiles. 'Morning!' each said to the other. The man's ebony forehead was furrowed, his eyes sad, making me wonder why he had travelled to England, apparently, from the other side of the world. His stance was that of teacher or doctor, rather than refuse collector. Was this the only work he could find to support family and growing grandchildren?

By the time we were ready to return to my mother's care home, the man was out of sight. I pushed her wheelchair along the uneven pavement, noticing him a few yards ahead. We caught up, smiled and I nodded in my mother's direction commenting, 'She's over 100 years old!'

Delight and respect swept across his face. He stuttered in broken English, 'In my country we'd ask someone as old as her to give us their blessing.' I could see that despite my mother's speechlessness, following a stroke, she understood our conversation and was gesticulating enthusiastically. 'Would you like her to do this for you?' I asked. His face glowed with pleasure as he dropped to his knees by her side. I gently lifted her paralysed hand and placed it on his head, and uttered words I knew she longed to say for herself, 'May God's richest blessing and love rest on you and yours, now and forever. Amen'. Three pairs of eyes brimmed over, as we went our separate ways.

It takes all sorts

Roger Combes

All kinds of people are involved when God is at work – and never more so than in those heady days after Pentecost, when the Holy Spirit and a few followers of Jesus launched the Christian church. 'God must like ordinary people, or he wouldn't have made so many of them,' says the T-shirt. These reflections highlight some of the men and women of different ages and backgrounds who make up the story of the early days of the church: a business woman, a prison officer, an absent-minded servant girl, a land owner, two leather-workers, the apostles Peter and Paul, and others. They are all valued, even special, individuals in the story of God's mission, as we are.

After the resurrection, the work of Jesus never stopped. People were still being healed and hearing the good news. People's hearts were being changed and finding peace. Jesus' followers were still suffering in a difficult world, but their Lord was unmistakably with them. And, as we consider the various characters and incidents in the story, each one sheds a light on our own lives: encouraging, challenging and inspiring us in our witness.

Acts 6:5, 8, 15 (NIV, abridged)

The face of an angel

They chose Stephen, a man full of faith and of the Holy Spirit… Now Stephen, a man full of God's grace and power, performed great wonders and signs among the people… All who were sitting in the Sanhedrin looked intently at Stephen, and they saw that his face was like the face of an angel.

We peer into the cot and see the baby fast asleep. 'Oh, the little angel,' we whisper.

Stephen, however, was an adult. The church had recently chosen him for a humble though important administrative job. We are told he was a man of wisdom, full of faith and full of God's grace and power. His work expanded, and soon opponents accused him of speaking of 'this Jesus of Nazareth' and against the law. Things turned nasty, but as the hard-nosed authorities looked at Stephen in the dock, soon to die at their hands, 'they saw that his face was like the face of an angel'. God's approval, or Stephen's innocence, was somehow shining through. Later Stephen says, 'I see heaven open and the Son of Man…'

Often our call to live for Christ can develop in unexpected ways, even to suffer. All pastors know that they have looked into the faces of God's saints on their hospital visits. The Christ of glory stands with us in our suffering, as he did with Stephen.

■ **PRAYER**

Lord of glory, thank you for going through suffering for me. Shine through me, so that others may see you in me today. Amen

Acts 9:10–11, 13, 15 (NIV, abridged)

A good contact

In Damascus there was a disciple named Ananias… The Lord told him, 'Go to the house of Judas on Straight Street and ask for a man from Tarsus named Saul, for he is praying.'… 'Lord,' Ananias answered, 'I have heard many reports about this man and all the harm he has done…' But the Lord said to Ananias, 'Go! This man is my chosen instrument to proclaim my name.'

In 1990, an apprentice mechanic was polishing cars, singing as he worked. A passing customer with connections in the music industry happened to hear him, and he gave him his card, suggesting that he go for an audition for training in London. He did and was accepted; and so began the successful career of a popular opera singer. (This is Alfie Boe, for those wondering!)

Ananias, a disciple in Damascus, was about to do the most significant thing in his life. He was uncomfortable about it, but the Lord insisted that he go to Saul, a violent man who had been persecuting believers. Saul was reeling from having just encountered the risen Christ on the Damascus road. Ananias eventually went, and his sympathetic and faithful contact with Saul, later Paul the apostle, was to set Saul's life on a new course, bringing the love of Christ to the world.

A small kindness and a courageous response at a key time can change the course of a person's life, at any stage in that life. Whatever our age, let us be alert to such opportunities.

■ PRAYER

Risen Christ, make me wise to where I can make a difference to someone else's life. Amen

Acts 9:32b–35 (NIV)

Jesus' work goes on

[Peter] went to visit the Lord's people who lived in Lydda. There he found a man named Aeneas, who was paralysed and had been bedridden for eight years. 'Aeneas,' Peter said to him, 'Jesus Christ heals you. Get up and roll up your mat.' Immediately Aeneas got up. All those who lived in Lydda and Sharon saw him and turned to the Lord.

Jesus often cared for 'ordinary' people and healed them, and here we find the apostle Peter in the countryside doing the same. He is at Lydda, a village near the coast – now Ben Gurion Airport – and in Christ's name he heals a man who has long been paralysed. Peter even echoes Jesus' famous words, 'Take up your bed and walk.' People were deeply impressed. Several times in Acts we read of many people 'turning to the Lord' and 'believing' because they saw Christ at work in local lives and homes.

So when a retired archbishop helps every week at a food bank, or when countless church members volunteer for their local hospices or give regularly to aid agencies – as they do – they are continuing to show Christ's love and care to 'ordinary people' and bearing witness to Christ in the wider community.

■ **PRAYER**

Lord Jesus Christ, thank you that your blessings are for all, and to you all people matter. May we reflect that truth in loving service and witness. Amen

Acts 11:5–9, 17 (NIV, abridged)

A big change of mind

'I saw a vision… [I] saw four-footed animals of the earth, wild beasts, reptiles and birds. Then I heard a voice telling me, "Get up, Peter. Kill and eat." I replied, "Surely not, Lord!…" The voice spoke from heaven a second time, "Do not call anything impure that God has made clean"… Who was I to think I could stand in God's way?'

The story of Ebenezer Scrooge in Charles Dickens' *A Christmas Carol* has a surprisingly happy ending. Scrooge changed. He rejected a lifetime of mean-spirited selfishness, and he came to delight in the fun of a family Christmas. He became a cheerful and generous benefactor.

Over the years, the apostle Peter had adopted some hard-line opinions and attitudes about certain people. For instance, he had always refused to enter the house of someone who was not Jewish. But God intervened with a vision that Peter could not get out of his mind, and then God sent him to a Roman centurion's house. Peter went, and his outlook changed. He saw that all people were to be treated the same and were worthy of the same gospel.

At different times in life, we, like Peter, can become rather fixed in our attitudes. This story challenges that, and shows that with God's help our minds and hearts can change.

■ **PRAYER**

'Spirit of the living God, fall afresh on me; break me, melt me, mould me, fill me.'* Amen

*Daniel Iverson (1890–1977)

Acts 11:20–23 (NIV, abridged)

Recognising God at work

Men from Cyprus and Cyrene went to Antioch and began to speak to Greeks also… A great number of people believed and turned to the Lord. News of this reached the church in Jerusalem, and they sent Barnabas to Antioch. When he arrived and saw what the grace of God had done, he was glad and encouraged them all to remain true to the Lord with all their hearts.

Before my parents were married, my father took his prospective wife to meet Bunty, a trusted relative. Afterwards, he was keen to know what Bunty thought of her. 'Well,' Bunty smiled, 'I'm not sure you're good enough for her.'

The leaders of the Jerusalem church wanted a second opinion about reports from Antioch, and they needed someone they could trust. To their credit, they chose Barnabas, a generous, big-hearted sort of person, who was particularly good at spotting God at work in people. So Barnabas went to the bustling city of Antioch, in present-day Syria. Remarkably, he saw significant numbers of Greeks and Romans responding to Jewish believers who were speaking about Jesus Christ. Although it was unprecedented, Barnabas was delighted. He recognised that it was the grace of God at work.

With God's help and at any age, we can learn to recognise the grace of God in other people, and see when God is doing something new.

■ **PRAYER**
Lord Jesus, make me like Barnabas, 'full of the Holy Spirit', seeing the grace of God in other people. Amen

Acts 12:13–14, 16–17a (NIV, abridged)

It takes all sorts

Peter knocked at the outer entrance, and a servant named Rhoda came to answer the door. When she recognised Peter's voice, she was so overjoyed she ran back without opening it and exclaimed, 'Peter is at the door!'... But Peter kept on knocking, and when they opened the door and saw him, they were astonished. Peter... described how the Lord had brought him out of prison.

Imagine Rhoda's surprise and delight if, years later, she were to hear this passage read out to the church. 'It's about me!'

Fancy the Bible mentioning a trivial incident like this: a servant named Rhoda answering the door, and, in her excitement, mistakenly leaving the apostle Peter in danger outside in the street. Amusing, perhaps – but Peter had just escaped from prison, and he quickly needed somewhere to hide from the authorities.

The other believers looked slightly foolish too. They had been praying that God would save Peter from prison; but when he did escape and stood in front of them, they did not believe it.

In our lifetime, most of us, like Rhoda, have made silly mistakes that could have been serious. But, praise God, he often overrules our foolishness, and he is still in charge. He can forgive our mistakes, and perhaps he allows himself the odd chuckle at our absent-mindedness.

■ **PRAYER**

We pray, Lord, for Christians across the world who are in prison or persecuted by the state. Please protect them and save them. Amen

Acts 16:14–15 (NIV, abridged)

Her heart opened

One of those listening was a woman… named Lydia, a dealer in purple cloth. She was a worshipper of God. The Lord opened her heart to respond to Paul's message. When she and the members of her household were baptised, she invited us to her home. 'If you consider me a believer in the Lord,' she said, 'come and stay at my house.' And she persuaded us.

Lydia was an independent businesswoman, selling high-end purple cloth. She was the head of her household, which was substantial enough to accommodate several guests and would become a base for the new church in Philippi. She was one of several women whom Paul met and spoke with in Philippi, in present-day northern Greece. They had gathered informally by the river.

This is the first time we read of the Christian gospel being spoken in Europe. As Lydia listened, a wonderful thing happened: 'The Lord opened her heart.' Lydia then welcomed baptism and invited Paul and his colleagues to stay. She was the hostess with the open heart.

There is no greater act of God than what he does in a human heart. It is one of his greatest miracles. Silently and unseen, he touches and warms and melts the hardest heart. It is why we keep praying for those we love, often for many years.

■ PRAYER
I praise you, Lord, for your mercy and power in opening my heart to yourself; graciously touch the hearts of those who resist you, I pray. Amen

Acts 16:32–34 (NIV)

A busy night

[Paul and Silas] spoke the word of the Lord to [the jailer] and to all the others in his house. At that hour of the night the jailer took them and washed their wounds; then immediately he and all his household were baptised. The jailer brought them into his house and set a meal before them; he was filled with joy because he had come to believe in God – he and his whole household.

It was a busy night for the jailer at Philippi. When he went to bed, all was quiet and all the prisoners were locked up. But the earthquake at midnight changed all that. This jailer, a conscientious government official, was desperate. His prisoners, though, did not flee, and that included Paul and Silas. Their message of Christ spoke to the jailer's heart and brought him comfort and hope. There and then, Paul baptised him, the gospel sign of cleansing from sin. Almost simultaneously, the jailer was cleansing Paul and Silas' wounds, which they had sustained in their flogging the day before. He kindly produced a meal in his home for Paul and Silas amid much joy. It was quite a night.

As with that jailer in Philippi, the consolation of Christ can still turn a dark night towards faith, joy and a concern for others.

■ PRAYER
We pray, Lord, for government workers, officials and civil servants: give them strength and sensitivity in their work, and may they bring compassion and practical help when dealing with their public. Amen

Acts 18:2–3, 24, 26 (NIV, abridged)

Pillars of the church

[Paul] met a Jew named Aquila… with his wife Priscilla… Paul went to see them, and because he was a tentmaker as they were, he stayed and worked with them… Meanwhile, a Jew named Apollos… began to speak boldly in the synagogue. When Priscilla and Aquila heard him, they invited him to their home and explained to him the way of God more adequately.

When my wife and I bought our house, we were surprised to discover it had an awning set in the back wall, which can be let down to provide shade when the patio is too hot. It is quite an asset.

Awnings for shops in Bible times would have been made by leather-workers, who would also make tents, sails and the like. This was the trade of Aquila and Priscilla, who were among the apostle Paul's closest associates in the gospel, particularly in big cities: Rome and, as here, Corinth and Ephesus. This Christian business couple were trusted and loved by the churches. They seem to have consistently provided a steady, guiding hand for individuals and Christian communities.

Older Christians behind the scenes can be of great value to a church or individual, offering, in an Aquila-Priscilla-like way, hospitality, gentle correction, a wise perspective or simply warm friendship.

■ PRAYER

Thank you, Lord, for those who are pillars of my church. Thank you for their steady support for the church's life in so many ways. Amen

Acts 20:22, 36–38 (NIV, abridged)

The wrench of goodbye

'And now, compelled by the Spirit, I am going to Jerusalem, not knowing what will happen to me there…' When Paul had finished speaking, he knelt down with all of them and prayed. They all wept as they embraced him and kissed him. What grieved them most was his statement that they would never see his face again. Then they accompanied him to the ship.

The farewell card says, 'Sorry you are going', and everyone in the office has signed it. They all get together and the boss says a warm thank you for the leaver's work. Then it's hugs, handshakes and best wishes for the future.

The nearest to a retirement 'do' that the apostle Paul came was a gathering of elders from Ephesus. As events were to turn out, Paul's days of exciting, free-ranging missionary work were over. Soon, he would always be a prisoner of some kind under someone else's control.

The wrench of leaving his main work behind must have been great. There were many tears as he said farewell. His responsibilities and circumstances were changing. But God still has tasks for retirees. As a prisoner, Paul still spoke up for the Lord Jesus, still helped others and, of course, still wrote letters – letters that would change the world.

■ PRAYER

We pray for those we know who are retiring at this time. As their responsibilities change, help them to know how best to serve you in the days ahead. Amen

Healing the family

Angela Tilby

These reflections are designed to help us to think through God's involvement in the life of our families. The Bible is utterly realistic about the human family. It recognises that biology matters. Parents and children are bonded together in ways that cannot be dissolved. But no human family is perfect. The Bible is full of accounts of families we might regard as dysfunctional, where there has been marital infidelity, violence, rejection and bitter rivalries between siblings.

Scripture suggests that broken families and irregular relationships are sometimes woven into the purposes of God. The family tree of the Messiah is full of such irregularities, and the conception of the Messiah by an unmarried virgin invites us to reflect on how God goes beyond human convention to bring salvation to the world.

As we approach the Christmas season, we might consider our own family relationships, giving thanks for what is good and life-giving and being ready to do our part in healing and reconciliation. We might also consider how we enable individuals to grow beyond what their families expect of them and how the challenge to leave our families for the sake of the gospel plays out in our own lives.

Ephesians 3:14–19 (NRSV)

Rooted and grounded in love

For this reason I bow my knees before the Father, from whom every family in heaven and on earth takes its name. I pray that, according to the riches of his glory, he may grant that you may be strengthened in your inner being with power through his Spirit, and that Christ may dwell in your hearts through faith, as you are being rooted and grounded in love. I pray that you may have the power to comprehend, with all the saints, what is the breadth and length and height and depth, and to know the love of Christ that surpasses knowledge, so that you may be filled with all the fullness of God.

No one is born into this world without a biological father and mother. Our parents are hugely influential on us, but our existence does not depend only on them. Parents are proxies for our ultimate parent, God. This is why Paul insists that whatever the circumstances of our birth and upbringing, our existence in this world is graced by God. The roots of fulfilment are in the immeasurable riches of God's love. This is not something we can earn. It is simply given, a daily invitation to grow more and more deeply into the mystery of God's love.

■ PRAYER

Father eternal, whatever I face today, let me know the love of Christ and the power of his Spirit, so that at the end of this day I may give glory to you. Amen

Genesis 3:20–24 (NRSV)

The Lord God clothed them

The man named his wife Eve, because she was the mother of all who live. And the Lord God made garments of skins for the man and for his wife, and clothed them. Then the Lord God said, 'See, the man has become like one of us, knowing good and evil; and now, he might reach out his hand and take also from the tree of life, and eat, and live forever' – therefore the Lord God sent him forth from the garden of Eden, to till the ground from which he was taken. He drove out the man; and at the east of the garden of Eden he placed the cherubim, and a sword flaming and turning to guard the way to the tree of life.

The story of Adam and Eve is the story of each one of us and of the human race collectively. It confronts us with our vulnerability. We may all have a dream of paradise, but our task in this world is to make our world both productive and a fit dwelling place for generations to come. God clothes Adam and Eve to protect them and then sends them out to work out what it is to be human in his world. This is our vocation: to learn to love and to work.

■ **PRAYER**

Lord God, may I know your protection this day. Guard me from temptation, and at my life's end show me once again the tree of life. Amen

Genesis 22:15–19 (NRSV)

Numerous as the stars

The angel of the Lord called to Abraham a second time from heaven, and said, 'By myself I have sworn, says the Lord: Because you have done this, and have not withheld your son, your only son, I will indeed bless you, and I will make your offspring as numerous as the stars of heaven and as the sand that is on the seashore. And your offspring shall possess the gate of their enemies, and by your offspring shall all the nations of the earth gain blessing for themselves, because you have obeyed my voice.' So Abraham returned to his young men, and they arose and went to Beer-sheba; and Abraham lived at Beer-sheba.

God blesses human family life, but we are not called to idolise the human family. Obedience to God is ultimately more important than even the closest biological ties. The testing of Abraham is a hard story, but the point is to reveal the depth of Abraham's faith in God. Like Mary the mother of Jesus, Abraham trusted God against the odds and God honoured that trust. His desire to bless the entire human race is dependent on the faith of individuals like you and me.

■ PRAYER
When I fear the future, Lord, show me again the stars of heaven and the sands of the seashore. Let me trust your promise to bring blessing, and give me the grace and strength to rejoice in what I do not yet see. Amen

Genesis 27:41–45 (NRSV)

Murderous intent

Now Esau hated Jacob because of the blessing with which his father had blessed him, and Esau said to himself, 'The days of mourning for my father are approaching; then I will kill my brother Jacob.' But the words of her elder son Esau were told to Rebekah; so she sent and called her younger son Jacob and said to him, 'Your brother Esau is consoling himself by planning to kill you. Now therefore, my son, obey my voice; flee at once to my brother Laban in Haran, and stay with him for a while, until your brother's fury turns away – until your brother's anger against you turns away, and he forgets what you have done to him; then I will send, and bring you back from there. Why should I lose both of you in one day?'

Families are seedbeds of the human future, but they can also be places of rivalry, cruelty and hatred. Jacob and Esau both have a divine vocation, but the strife between them has the potential to wreck both their lives. The parents too are at fault. Rebekah has favoured Jacob and encouraged his ambitious nature. She now, wisely, tells Jacob to flee. Time and distance are sometimes necessary for a broken relationship to have a chance to heal.

■ PRAYER

Lord, I pray for any in my family who are estranged from one another. Let time and distance calm anger and make space for future peace. Amen

Genesis 33:1–4, 8–10 (NRSV)

The face of God

Now Jacob looked up and saw Esau coming, and four hundred men with him. So he divided the children among Leah and Rachel and the two maids. He put the maids with their children in front, then Leah with her children, and Rachel and Joseph last of all. He himself went on ahead of them, bowing himself to the ground seven times, until he came near his brother. But Esau ran to meet him, and embraced him, and fell on his neck and kissed him, and they wept… Esau said, 'What do you mean by all this company that I met?' Jacob answered, 'To find favour with my lord.' But Esau said, 'I have enough, my brother; keep what you have for yourself.' Jacob said, 'No, please; if I find favour with you, then accept my present from my hand; for truly to see your face is like seeing the face of God – since you have received me with such favour.'

Reconciliation in families is not impossible, but it is costly. Jacob has fought with the angel at the ford of Jabbok (Genesis 33) and he has been wounded. He is now ready to approach the brother he has wronged. He comes with gifts. But more important, he recognises him as one who reflects the divine likeness. He is more than a biological brother – he is a child of God.

■ PRAYER

Lord, may I see your face in all who I meet this day, especially in those who challenge me. Amen

Matthew 1:1–6a (NRSV)

Reading the family tree

An account of the genealogy of Jesus the Messiah, the son of David, the son of Abraham. Abraham was the father of Isaac, and Isaac the father of Jacob, and Jacob the father of Judah and his brothers, and Judah the father of Perez and Zerah by Tamar, and Perez the father of Hezron, and Hezron the father of Aram, and Aram the father of Aminadab, and Aminadab the father of Nahshon, and Nahshon the father of Salmon, and Salmon the father of Boaz by Rahab, and Boaz the father of Obed by Ruth, and Obed the father of Jesse, and Jesse the father of King David.

Jesus was 'born of David's line'. But what an extraordinary family tree it is. Betrayal, rape and prostitution are part of the family story: Tamar, Rahab and Ruth all represent sexual 'outsiders'. When God became incarnate in Christ by the Holy Spirit and the virgin Mary, he took on the human family with all its complexities and irregularities. There is sin in the Messiah's ancestry, but it is sin that is redeemed. At Christmas, we celebrate our redemption in the sign of the young virgin who miraculously gives birth to the Son of God. Our family secrets can shame us, or help remake us.

■ **PRAYER**
Lord, as we reflect on the past, our families and their history, help us to see clearly both the sin and the grace, and have confidence in your healing Spirit. Amen

Matthew 1:18–21 (NRSV)

As it was in the beginning

Now the birth of Jesus the Messiah took place in this way. When his mother Mary had been engaged to Joseph, but before they lived together, she was found to be with child from the Holy Spirit. Her husband Joseph, being a righteous man and unwilling to expose her to public disgrace, planned to dismiss her quietly. But just when he had resolved to do this, an angel of the Lord appeared to him in a dream and said, 'Joseph, son of David, do not be afraid to take Mary as your wife, for the child conceived in her is from the Holy Spirit. She will bear a son, and you are to name him Jesus, for he will save his people from their sins.'

The Christmas season is often a complicated time for families; the best and worst of family life are on display. There are also those who are lonely at this time, whose families have died or moved away and who can feel forgotten. For many, the Christmas festival is bittersweet. Yet we know deep down that Christmas calls out for generosity of spirit. We can be gracious, as Joseph was, giving each other the benefit of the doubt and looking to God to astonish us with his presence in the needy and in strangers. Christ has ever new ways of showing us we are saved from our sins.

■ **PRAYER**

Lord, may we worship you, the Word made flesh, born for our salvation. Amen

Luke 2:42–46, 48–49 (NRSV)

In the Father's house

When [Jesus] was twelve years old, they went up as usual for the festival. When the festival was ended and they started to return, the boy Jesus stayed behind in Jerusalem, but his parents did not know it. Assuming that he was in the group of travellers, they went a day's journey. Then they started to look for him among their relatives and friends. When they did not find him, they returned to Jerusalem to search for him. After three days they found him in the temple, sitting among the teachers, listening to them and asking them questions… When his parents saw him they were astonished; and his mother said to him, 'Child, why have you treated us like this? Look, your father and I have been searching for you in great anxiety.' He said to them, 'Why were you searching for me? Did you not know that I must be in my Father's house?'

This is a hard story for any anxious parent. The loss of a child is a terrible anxiety, and we should not read Jesus' answer as a rebuke to those parents who rightly worry about their children. But Christ's perspective is always wider than ours. The human family nourishes us, not because it rivals our deep relatedness to God, but because it makes space for it. We are all to find our true maturity within our Father's house.

■ PRAYER
Lord, may I dwell in your house forever. Amen

Mark 10:28–32a (NRSV)

For the sake of the gospel

Peter began to say to [Jesus], 'Look, we have left everything and followed you.' Jesus said, 'Truly I tell you, there is no one who has left house or brothers or sisters or mother or father or children or fields, for my sake and for the sake of the good news, who will not receive a hundredfold now in this age – houses, brothers and sisters, mothers and children, and fields, with persecutions – and in the age to come eternal life. But many who are first will be last, and the last will be first.' They were on the road, going up to Jerusalem.

The call of Jesus is a call to conversion. Those who follow him set aside their old way of life and take on new priorities. Not all are called literally to leave their families, but all are called to live the Christian faith in company with others and to witness to their faith in a world that can sometimes be hostile. Jesus' demand to 'leave everything' can seem harsh, but it is also a potential liberation. Even the best of families is limited in its perception of its members. There is a point at which we need to allow ourselves to be led by the Spirit into the fullness of life God desires for us.

■ **PRAYER**
Lord of the journey, help me to trust you that what I sacrifice for your name's sake will bear fruit in your kingdom. Amen

Matthew 6:7–13 (NRSV)

The prayer of Jesus

'When you are praying, do not heap up empty phrases as the Gentiles do; for they think that they will be heard because of their many words. Do not be like them, for your Father knows what you need before you ask him. Pray then in this way: Our Father in heaven, hallowed be your name. Your kingdom come. Your will be done, on earth as it is in heaven. Give us this day our daily bread. And forgive us our debts, as we also have forgiven our debtors. And do not bring us to the time of trial, but rescue us from the evil one.'

There is nothing mysterious about the Lord's Prayer. It is the kind of prayer every Jew of Jesus' time would have been familiar with. What is significant for us is that the prayer is given by Jesus. It is an invitation to pray as part of his family, as one of his brothers or sisters. This prayer is one of the most important gifts to be passed on within the Christian family. Not too short to be trivial, not too long to be remembered, these words bind us to Christ, to his promise, to his Spirit, to his faith in the Father. It is a prayer for the family to say together and for each individual to know by heart.

■ PRAYER

Father, send your Spirit into our hearts that we may not only call you Father, but know you as Lord and God. Amen

Help us raise God-connected children and teens through a gift in your will

Aged twelve, Jesus went with his family to Jerusalem to celebrate the Feast of Passover. After the festival, the family began their journey home, but Jesus was not among them. He stayed behind 'in the temple courts, sitting among the teachers, listening to them and asking them questions' (Luke 2:46, NIV).

It's a picture that may sound familiar to some parents. Perhaps you can remember a time when you were trying to get your kids ready for school, a family meal or another engagement. There was much to do and time was slipping away, but all your kids wanted to do was ask questions about anything and everything.

As a parent, you often want to encourage your children to ask questions, spiritual or otherwise, so that they can learn and discover new things. But life must go on and those shoe laces won't tie themselves! It's a tricky predicament.

Our Parenting for Faith team understands this dichotomy. They aim to equip parents and carers to confidently parent for faith in the midst of the mundane: when ferrying the children back and forth, sitting on the bathroom floor potty-training toddlers or waving kids off on their first day of secondary school.

Through their website, an eight-session course and numerous events and training opportunities, the Parenting for Faith team are helping Christian parents raise God-connected children and teens. They're helping to raise a new generation that can bring God's love to a world in need.

Could you help this work continue by leaving a gift in your will? Even a small amount can help make a lasting difference in the lives of parents and children.

For further information about making a gift to BRF in your will, please visit **brf.org.uk/lastingdifference**, contact **+44 (0)1865 319700** or email **giving@brf.org.uk**.

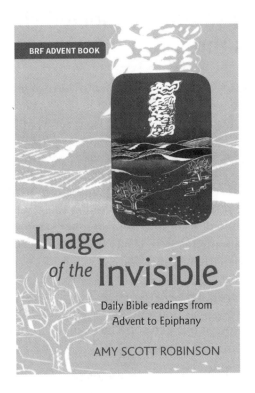

As we look towards celebrating the incarnation at Christmas, we consider how God chose to express himself, in a moment in history, as a tiny baby. But what other images describe God in the Bible, and what can we learn about his character through them? How does an invisible God reveal himself to us in scripture and in Jesus? Amy Scott Robinson, a poet and storyteller, answers this question with imagination and a close reading of the text.

Image of the Invisible
Daily Bible readings from Advent to Epiphany
Amy Scott Robinson
978 0 85746 789 8   £8.99
brfonline.org.uk

From the author of *Postcards from Heaven* comes this unusual and beautiful gift. *Postcards of Hope* is a collection of original, beautiful watercolours by Ellie Hart, each with a short reflection aimed at helping the reader hear from God. For the tired and weary and those who want to have God breathe new life into their relationship with him.

Postcards of Hope
Words and pictures to breathe life into your heart
Ellie Hart
978 0 85746 648 8 £8.99
brfonline.org.uk

To order

Online: **brfonline.org.uk**
Telephone: +44 (0)1865 319700
Mon–Fri 9.15–17.30
Post: complete this form and send to the address below

Delivery times within the UK are normally 15 working days. Prices are correct at the time of going to press but may change without prior notice.

Title	Issue*	Price	Qty	Total
Image of the Invisible		£8.99		
Postcards of Hope		£8.99		
Bible Reflections for Older People (single copy)	Sep 19/Jan 20*	£5.05		

*delete as appropriate

POSTAGE AND PACKING CHARGES			
Order value	UK	Europe	Rest of world
Under £7.00	£2.00	available on request	available on request
£7.00–£29.99	£3.00	available on request	available on request
£30.00 and over	FREE	available on request	available on request

Total value of books	
Postage and packing	
Total for this order	

Please complete in BLOCK CAPITALS

Title .... First name/initials .... Surname ....

Address ....

.... Postcode ....

Acc. No. .... Telephone ....

Email ....

Method of payment

☐ Cheque (made payable to BRF) ☐ MasterCard / Visa

Card no. ☐☐☐☐ ☐☐☐☐ ☐☐☐☐ ☐☐☐☐

Expires end ☐☐ ☐☐ Security code* ☐☐☐ Last 3 digits on the reverse of the card

Signature* .... Date .... /............ /............
*ESSENTIAL IN ORDER TO PROCESS YOUR ORDER

Please return this form to:

BRF, 15 The Chambers, Vineyard, Abingdon OX14 3FE | enquiries@brf.org.uk
To read our terms and conditions, please visit **brfonline.org.uk/terms**.

BROP0319   The Bible Reading Fellowship (BRF) is a Registered Charity (233280)

BIBLE REFLECTIONS FOR OLDER PEOPLE GROUP SUBSCRIPTION FORM

> All our Bible reading notes can be ordered online
> by visiting **biblereadingnotes.org.uk/subscriptions**

The group subscription rate for *Bible Reflections for Older People* will be £15.15 per person until April 2019.

☐ I would like to take out a group subscription for .... (*quantity*) copies.

☐ Please start my order with the January 2020 / May 2020 / September 2020* issue.
I would like to pay annually/receive an invoice with each edition of the notes.* (*delete as appropriate*)

Please do not send any money with your order. Send your order to BRF and we will send you an invoice. The group subscription year is from 1 May to 30 April. If you start subscribing in the middle of a subscription year we will invoice you for the remaining number of issues left in that year.

Name and address of the person organising the group subscription:

Title .... First name/initials .... Surname...

Address...

.... Postcode ....

Telephone .... Email..

Church...

Name of minister ....

Name and address of the person paying the invoice if the invoice needs to be sent directly to them:

Title .... First name/initials .... Surname...

Address...

.... Postcode ....

Telephone .... Email..

Please return this form to:
BRF, 15 The Chambers, Vineyard, Abingdon OX14 3FE | enquiries@brf.org.uk
To read our terms and conditions, please visit **brfonline.org.uk/terms**.

BROP0319   The Bible Reading Fellowship is a Registered Charity (233280)

BIBLE REFLECTIONS FOR OLDER PEOPLE INDIVIDUAL/GIFT SUBSCRIPTION FORM

To order online, please visit **biblereadingnotes.org.uk/subscriptions**

☐ I would like to take out a subscription (*complete your name and address details only once*)
☐ I would like to give a gift subscription (*please provide both names and addresses*)

Title .... First name/initials .... Surname ....

Address ....

.... Postcode ....

Telephone .... Email ....

Gift subscription name ....

Gift subscription address ....

.... Postcode ....

Gift message (*20 words max. or include your own gift card*):

....

....

Please send **Bible Reflections for Older People** beginning with the January 2020 / May 2020 / September 2020* issue (**delete as appropriate*):

(*please tick box*)	UK	Europe	Rest of world
Bible Reflections for Older People	☐ £19.20	☐ £27.00	☐ £31.05

Total enclosed £ .... (*cheques should be made payable to 'BRF'*)

Please charge my MasterCard / Visa ☐ Debit card ☐ with £ ....

Card no. ☐☐☐☐ ☐☐☐☐ ☐☐☐☐ ☐☐☐☐

Expires end ☐☐☐☐ Security code* ☐☐☐ Last 3 digits on the reverse of the card

Signature* .... Date ..../......./.......

*ESSENTIAL IN ORDER TO PROCESS YOUR ORDER

Please return this form to:
BRF, 15 The Chambers, Vineyard, Abingdon OX14 3FE | enquiries@brf.org.uk
To read our terms and conditions, please visit **brfonline.org.uk/terms**.

The Bible Reading Fellowship is a Registered Charity (233280)